INFORMATIONS

NAME

ADDRESS

E-MAIL ADDRESS

WEBSITE

PHONE **FAX**

EMERGENCY CONTACT PERSON

PHONE **FAX**

Hiking Notes

Date ....

Start Time .... End Time ....

Weather ☀️ ☁️ 🌧️❄️ Temp ....

Location / Park ....

Distance .... Duration ....

Trails ....

Elevation Gain / Loss ....

Terrain ....

Difficulty   Easy   1   2   3   4   5   6   Hard

Companions

....

....

Cost / Fees

....

Facilities

....

Cell Reception / Carrier ....

NATURE / WILDLIFE OBSERVED

....

....

....

....

Hiking rate   ⭐ ⭐ ⭐ ⭐ ⭐

Hiking Notes

....
....
....
....
....
....
....
....
....
....
....
....
....
....
....
....
....
....
....
....
....
....
....
....
....

Hiking Notes

Date ....

Start Time .... End Time ....

Weather ☀ ☁ 🌧❄ Temp ....

Location / Park ....

Distance .... Duration ....

Trails ....

Elevation Gain / Loss ....

Terrain ....

Difficulty   Easy   1   2   3   4   5   6   Hard

Companions
....
....

Cost/ Fees
....

Facilities
....

Cell Reception / Carrier ....

NATURE / WILDLIFE OBSERVED
....
....
....
....

Hiking rate   ⭐ ⭐ ⭐ ⭐ ⭐

 # Hiking Notes

....
....
....
....
....
....
....
....
....
....
....
....
....
....
....
....
....
....
....
....
....
....
....
....
....
....
....
....

Hiking Notes

Date ....

Start Time .... End Time ....

Weather ☀ ☁ 🌧 Temp ....

Location / Park ....

Distance .... Duration ....

Trails ....

Elevation Gain / Loss ....

Terrain ....

Difficulty   Easy   1   2   3   4   5   6   Hard

Companions
....
....

Cost/ Fees
....

Facilities
....

Cell Reception / Carrier ....

NATURE / WILDLIFE OBSERVED

....
....
....
....

Hiking rate ☆ ☆ ☆ ☆ ☆

 # Hiking Notes

Hiking Notes

Date ....

Start Time .... End Time ....

Weather ☀ ☁ 🌧❄ Temp ....

Location / Park ....

Distance .... Duration ....

Trails ....

Elevation Gain / Loss ....

Terrain ....

Difficulty   Easy   1   2   3   4   5   6   Hard

Companions
....
....

Cost / Fees
....

Facilities
....

Cell Reception / Carrier ....

NATURE / WILDLIFE OBSERVED

....
....
....
....

Hiking rate   ⭐ ⭐ ⭐ ⭐ ⭐

Hiking Notes

Hiking Notes

Date ....

Start Time .... End Time ....

Weather ☀️ ☁️ 🌧️❄️ Temp ....

Location / Park ....

Distance .... Duration ....

Trails ....

Elevation Gain / Loss ....

Terrain ....

Difficulty   Easy   1   2   3   4   5   6   Hard

Companions

....

....

Cost / Fees

....

Facilities

....

Cell Reception / Carrier ....

NATURE / WILDLIFE OBSERVED

....

....

....

....

Hiking rate ⭐ ⭐ ⭐ ⭐ ⭐

Hiking Notes

....
....
....
....
....
....
....
....
....
....
....
....
....
....
....
....
....
....
....
....
....
....
....
....

Hiking Notes

Date ....

Start Time .... End Time ....

Weather ☀ ☁ 🌧❄ Temp ....

Location / Park ....

Distance .... Duration ....

Trails ....

Elevation Gain / Loss ....

Terrain ....

Difficulty Easy 1 2 3 4 5 6 Hard

Companions
....
....

Cost/ Fees
....

Facilities
....

Cell Reception / Carrier ....

NATURE / WILDLIFE OBSERVED

....
....
....
....

Hiking rate ⭐ ⭐ ⭐ ⭐ ⭐

 # Hiking Notes

....
....
....
....
....
....
....
....
....
....
....
....
....
....
....
....
....
....
....
....
....
....
....
....
....

Hiking Notes

Date ....

Start Time .... End Time ....

Weather ☀️ ☁️ 🌧️ Temp ....

Location / Park ....

Distance .... Duration ....

Trails ....

Elevation Gain / Loss ....

Terrain ....

Difficulty   Easy   1   2   3   4   5   6   Hard

Companions
....
....

Cost / Fees
....

Facilities
....

Cell Reception / Carrier ....

NATURE / WILDLIFE OBSERVED

....
....
....
....

Hiking rate ⭐ ⭐ ⭐ ⭐ ⭐

Hiking Notes

....
....
....
....
....
....
....
....
....
....
....
....
....
....
....
....
....
....
....
....
....
....
....
....

Hiking Notes

Date ....

Start Time .... End Time ....

Weather ☀️ ☁️ 🌧️ Temp ....

Location / Park ....

Distance .... Duration ....

Trails ....

Elevation Gain / Loss ....

Terrain ....

Difficulty   Easy   1   2   3   4   5   6   Hard

Companions
....
....

Cost / Fees
....

Facilities
....

Cell Reception / Carrier ....

NATURE / WILDLIFE OBSERVED

....
....
....
....

Hiking rate ⭐ ⭐ ⭐ ⭐ ⭐

Hiking Notes

....

....

....

....

....

....

....

....

....

....

....

....

....

....

....

....

....

....

....

....

....

....

....

....

....

....

....

Hiking Notes

Date ....

Start Time .... End Time ....

Weather ☀ ☁ 🌧 Temp ....

Location / Park ....

Distance .... Duration ....

Trails ....

Elevation Gain / Loss ....

Terrain ....

Difficulty Easy 1 2 3 4 5 6 Hard

Companions

....

....

Cost / Fees

....

Facilities

....

Cell Reception / Carrier ....

NATURE / WILDLIFE OBSERVED

....

....

....

....

Hiking rate ⭐ ⭐ ⭐ ⭐ ⭐

Hiking Notes

Hiking Notes

Date ....

Start Time .... End Time ....

Weather ☀ ⛅ 🌧 Temp ....

Location / Park ....

Distance .... Duration ....

Trails ....

Elevation Gain / Loss ....

Terrain ....

Difficulty Easy 1 2 3 4 5 6 Hard

Companions

....

....

Cost / Fees

....

Facilities

....

Cell Reception / Carrier ....

NATURE / WILDLIFE OBSERVED

....

....

....

....

Hiking rate ☆ ☆ ☆ ☆ ☆

Hiking Notes

Hiking Notes

Date ....

Start Time .... End Time ....

Weather ☀ ☁ 🌧 Temp ....

Location / Park ....

Distance .... Duration

Trails ....

Elevation Gain / Loss ....

Terrain ....

Difficulty   Easy   1   2   3   4   5   6   Hard

Companions
....
....

Cost / Fees
....

Facilities
....

Cell Reception / Carrier ....

NATURE / WILDLIFE OBSERVED
....
....
....
....

Hiking rate   ★ ★ ★ ★ ★

Hiking Notes

....
....
....
....
....
....
....
....
....
....
....
....
....
....
....
....
....
....
....
....
....
....
....

Hiking Notes

Date ....

Start Time .... **End Time** ....

Weather ☀ ☁ 🌧 **Temp** ....

Location / Park ....

Distance .... **Duration** ....

Trails ....

Elevation Gain / Loss ....

Terrain ....

Difficulty Easy 1 2 3 4 5 6 Hard

Companions

....

....

Cost / Fees

....

Facilities

....

Cell Reception / Carrier ....

NATURE / WILDLIFE OBSERVED

....

....

....

....

Hiking rate ⭐ ⭐ ⭐ ⭐ ⭐

Hiking Notes

Hiking Notes

Date ....

Start Time .... End Time ....

Weather ☀ ☁ 🌧 Temp ....

Location / Park ....

Distance .... Duration ....

Trails ....

Elevation Gain / Loss ....

Terrain ....

Difficulty   Easy   1   2   3   4   5   6   Hard

Companions
....
....

Cost / Fees
....

Facilities
....

Cell Reception / Carrier ....

NATURE / WILDLIFE OBSERVED
....
....
....
....

Hiking rate   ⭐ ⭐ ⭐ ⭐ ⭐

 # Hiking Notes

....
....
....
....
....
....
....
....
....
....
....
....
....
....
....
....
....
....
....
....
....
....
....
....
....

Hiking Notes

Date ....

Start Time .... End Time ....

Weather ☀ ☁ 🌧 Temp ....

Location / Park ....

Distance .... Duration ....

Trails ....

Elevation Gain / Loss ....

Terrain ....

Difficulty   Easy   1   2   3   4   5   6   Hard

Companions
....
....

Cost / Fees
....

Facilities
....

Cell Reception / Carrier ....

NATURE / WILDLIFE OBSERVED
....
....
....
....

Hiking rate   ☆ ☆ ☆ ☆ ☆

Hiking Notes

....

....

....

....

....

....

....

....

....

....

....

....

....

....

....

....

....

....

....

....

....

....

Hiking Notes

Date ....

Start Time .... End Time ....

Weather ☀ ☁ 🌧❄ Temp ....

Location / Park ....

Distance .... Duration ....

Trails ....

Elevation Gain / Loss ....

Terrain ....

Difficulty   Easy   1   2   3   4   5   6   Hard

Companions

....

....

Cost / Fees

....

Facilities

....

Cell Reception / Carrier ....

NATURE / WILDLIFE OBSERVED

....

....

....

....

Hiking rate   ⭐ ⭐ ⭐ ⭐ ⭐

 # Hiking Notes

....

....

....

....

....

....

....

....

....

....

....

....

....

....

....

....

....

....

....

....

....

....

....

Hiking Notes

Date ....

Start Time .... **End Time** ....

Weather ☀️ ☁️ 🌧️ **Temp** ....

Location / Park ....

Distance .... **Duration** ....

Trails ....

Elevation Gain / Loss ....

Terrain ....

Difficulty   Easy   1   2   3   4   5   6   Hard

Companions

....

....

Cost / Fees

....

Facilities

....

Cell Reception / Carrier ....

NATURE / WILDLIFE OBSERVED

....

....

....

....

Hiking rate   ⭐ ⭐ ⭐ ⭐ ⭐

 # Hiking Notes

....

....

....

....

....

....

....

....

....

....

....

....

....

....

....

....

....

....

....

....

....

....

....

Hiking Notes

Date ....

Start Time .... End Time ....

Weather ☀ ☁ ⛆ Temp ....

Location / Park ....

Distance .... Duration ....

Trails ....

Elevation Gain / Loss ....

Terrain ....

Difficulty   Easy   1   2   3   4   5   6   Hard

Companions

....

....

Cost / Fees

....

Facilities

....

Cell Reception / Carrier ....

NATURE / WILDLIFE OBSERVED

....

....

....

....

Hiking rate ★ ★ ★ ★ ★

Hiking Notes

Hiking Notes

Date ....

Start Time .... End Time ....

Weather ☀️ ☁️ 🌧️ Temp ....

Location / Park ....

Distance .... Duration ....

Trails ....

Elevation Gain / Loss ....

Terrain ....

Difficulty   Easy   1   2   3   4   5   6   Hard

Companions

....
....

Cost/ Fees

....

Facilities

....

Cell Reception / Carrier ....

NATURE / WILDLIFE OBSERVED

....
....
....
....

Hiking rate   ⭐ ⭐ ⭐ ⭐ ⭐

Hiking Notes

....
....
....
....
....
....
....
....
....
....
....
....
....
....
....
....
....
....
....
....
....
....
....

Hiking Notes

Date ....

Start Time .... End Time ....

Weather ☀ ☁ 🌧 Temp ....

Location / Park ....

Distance .... Duration ....

Trails ....

Elevation Gain / Loss ....

Terrain ....

Difficulty   Easy   1   2   3   4   5   6   Hard

Companions
....
....

Cost / Fees
....

Facilities
....

Cell Reception / Carrier ....

NATURE / WILDLIFE OBSERVED

....
....
....
....

Hiking rate ⭐ ⭐ ⭐ ⭐ ⭐

Hiking Notes

Hiking Notes

Date ....

Start Time .... End Time ....

Weather ☀ ☁ 🌧❄ Temp ....

Location / Park ....

Distance .... Duration ....

Trails ....

Elevation Gain / Loss ....

Terrain ....

Difficulty   Easy   1   2   3   4   5   6   Hard

Companions
....
....

Cost/ Fees
....

Facilities
....

Cell Reception / Carrier ....

NATURE / WILDLIFE OBSERVED

....
....
....
....

Hiking rate   ⭐ ⭐ ⭐ ⭐ ⭐

Hiking Notes

Hiking Notes

Date ....

Start Time .... End Time ....

Weather ☀️ ☁️ 🌧️ Temp ....

Location / Park ....

Distance .... Duration ....

Trails ....

Elevation Gain / Loss ....

Terrain ....

Difficulty   Easy   1   2   3   4   5   6   Hard

Companions
....
....

Cost / Fees
....

Facilities
....

Cell Reception / Carrier ....

NATURE / WILDLIFE OBSERVED

....
....
....
....

Hiking rate   ⭐ ⭐ ⭐ ⭐ ⭐

Hiking Notes

Hiking Notes

Date ....

Start Time .... End Time ....

Weather ☀ ☁ 🌧 Temp ....

Location / Park ....

Distance .... Duration ....

Trails ....

Elevation Gain / Loss ....

Terrain ....

Difficulty   Easy   1   2   3   4   5   6   Hard

Companions
....
....

Cost / Fees
....

Facilities
....

Cell Reception / Carrier ....

NATURE / WILDLIFE OBSERVED

....
....
....
....

Hiking rate ⭐ ⭐ ⭐ ⭐ ⭐

Hiking Notes

Hiking Notes

Date ....

Start Time .... End Time ....

Weather ☀ ☁ 🌧❄ Temp ....

Location / Park ....

Distance .... Duration ....

Trails ....

Elevation Gain / Loss ....

Terrain ....

Difficulty   Easy   1   2   3   4   5   6   Hard

Companions
....
....

Cost / Fees
....

Facilities
....

Cell Reception / Carrier ....

NATURE / WILDLIFE OBSERVED

....
....
....
....

Hiking rate   ★ ★ ★ ★ ★

Hiking Notes

....

....

....

....

....

....

....

....

....

....

....

....

....

....

....

....

....

....

....

....

....

....

....

....

Hiking Notes

Date ....

Start Time .... End Time ....

Weather ☀ ☁ 🌧 Temp ....

Location / Park ....

Distance .... Duration ....

Trails ....

Elevation Gain / Loss ....

Terrain ....

Difficulty   Easy   1   2   3   4   5   6   Hard

Companions
....
....

Cost / Fees
....

Facilities
....

Cell Reception / Carrier ....

NATURE / WILDLIFE OBSERVED
....
....
....
....

Hiking rate ☆ ☆ ☆ ☆ ☆

 # Hiking Notes

....
....
....
....
....
....
....
....
....
....
....
....
....
....
....
....
....
....
....
....
....
....
....

Hiking Notes

Date ....

Start Time .... **End Time** ....

Weather ☀ ☁ 🌧 **Temp** ....

Location / Park ....

Distance .... **Duration** ....

Trails ....

Elevation Gain / Loss ....

Terrain ....

Difficulty   Easy   1   2   3   4   5   6   Hard

Companions

....

....

Cost/ Fees

....

Facilities

....

Cell Reception / Carrier ....

NATURE / WILDLIFE OBSERVED

....

....

....

....

Hiking rate   ⭐ ⭐ ⭐ ⭐ ⭐

Hiking Notes

Hiking Notes

Date ....

Start Time .... End Time ....

Weather ☀ ⛅ 🌧❄ Temp ....

Location / Park ....

Distance .... Duration ....

Trails ....

Elevation Gain / Loss ....

Terrain ....

Difficulty   Easy   1   2   3   4   5   6   Hard

Companions

....

....

Cost/ Fees

....

Facilities

....

Cell Reception / Carrier ....

NATURE / WILDLIFE OBSERVED

....
....
....
....

Hiking rate ⭐ ⭐ ⭐ ⭐ ⭐

Hiking Notes

Hiking Notes

Date ....

Start Time .... End Time ....

Weather ☼ ☁ 🌧 Temp ....

Location / Park ....

Distance .... Duration ....

Trails ....

Elevation Gain / Loss ....

Terrain ....

Difficulty   Easy   1   2   3   4   5   6   Hard

Companions
....
....

Cost / Fees
....

Facilities
....

Cell Reception / Carrier ....

NATURE / WILDLIFE OBSERVED

....
....
....
....

Hiking rate ⭐ ⭐ ⭐ ⭐ ⭐

Hiking Notes

....
....
....
....
....
....
....
....
....
....
....
....
....
....
....
....
....
....
....
....
....
....
....
....

Hiking Notes

Date ....

Start Time .... End Time ....

Weather ☀️ ☁️ 🌧️❄️ Temp ....

Location / Park ....

Distance .... Duration ....

Trails ....

Elevation Gain / Loss ....

Terrain ....

Difficulty   Easy   1   2   3   4   5   6   Hard

Companions

....

....

Cost / Fees

....

Facilities

....

Cell Reception / Carrier ....

NATURE / WILDLIFE OBSERVED

....

....

....

....

Hiking rate   ⭐ ⭐ ⭐ ⭐ ⭐

 # Hiking Notes

Hiking Notes

Date ....

Start Time .... End Time ....

Weather ☀ ☁ 🌧❄ Temp ....

Location / Park ....

Distance .... Duration ....

Trails ....

Elevation Gain / Loss ....

Terrain ....

Difficulty   Easy   1   2   3   4   5   6   Hard

Companions
....
....

Cost / Fees
....

Facilities
....

Cell Reception / Carrier ....

NATURE / WILDLIFE OBSERVED
....
....
....
....

Hiking rate   ⭐ ⭐ ⭐ ⭐ ⭐

 # Hiking Notes

....

....

....

....

....

....

....

....

....

....

....

....

....

....

....

....

....

....

....

....

....

....

Hiking Notes

Date ....

Start Time .... End Time ....

Weather ☀ ☁ 🌧 Temp ....

Location / Park ....

Distance .... Duration ....

Trails ....

Elevation Gain / Loss ....

Terrain ....

Difficulty   Easy   1   2   3   4   5   6   Hard

Companions
....
....

Cost/ Fees
....

Facilities
....

Cell Reception / Carrier ....

NATURE / WILDLIFE OBSERVED

....
....
....
....

Hiking rate   ⭐ ⭐ ⭐ ⭐ ⭐

 # Hiking Notes

....
....
....
....
....
....
....
....
....
....
....
....
....
....
....
....
....
....
....
....
....
....
....
....

Hiking Notes

Date ....

Start Time .... End Time ....

Weather ☀ ☁ 🌧❄ Temp ....

Location / Park ....

Distance .... Duration ....

Trails ....

Elevation Gain / Loss ....

Terrain ....

Difficulty   Easy   1   2   3   4   5   6   Hard

Companions

....

....

Cost / Fees

....

Facilities

....

Cell Reception / Carrier ....

NATURE / WILDLIFE OBSERVED

....

....

....

....

Hiking rate   ⭐ ⭐ ⭐ ⭐ ⭐

Hiking Notes

Hiking Notes

Date ....

Start Time .... End Time ....

Weather ☀ ☁ 🌧 Temp ....

Location / Park ....

Distance .... Duration ....

Trails ....

Elevation Gain / Loss ....

Terrain ....

Difficulty   Easy   1   2   3   4   5   6   Hard

Companions
....
....

Cost / Fees
....

Facilities
....

Cell Reception / Carrier ....

NATURE / WILDLIFE OBSERVED

....
....
....
....

Hiking rate   ☆ ☆ ☆ ☆ ☆

Hiking Notes

Hiking Notes

Date ....

Start Time .... End Time ....

Weather ☀ ☁ 🌧 Temp ....

Location / Park ....

Distance .... Duration ....

Trails ....

Elevation Gain / Loss ....

Terrain ....

Difficulty   Easy   1   2   3   4   5   6   Hard

Companions

....

....

Cost / Fees

....

Facilities

....

Cell Reception / Carrier ....

NATURE / WILDLIFE OBSERVED

....

....

....

....

Hiking rate   ★ ★ ★ ★ ★

 # Hiking Notes

....

....

....

....

....

....

....

....

....

....

....

....

....

....

....

....

....

....

....

....

....

....

....

....

....

....

Hiking Notes

Date ....

Start Time .... End Time ....

Weather ☀ ☁ 🌧 Temp ....

Location / Park ....

Distance .... Duration ....

Trails ....

Elevation Gain / Loss ....

Terrain ....

Difficulty   Easy   1   2   3   4   5   6   Hard

Companions
....
....

Cost / Fees
....

Facilities
....

Cell Reception / Carrier ....

NATURE / WILDLIFE OBSERVED

....
....
....
....

Hiking rate   ⭐ ⭐ ⭐ ⭐ ⭐

Hiking Notes

Hiking Notes

Date ....

Start Time .... End Time ....

Weather ☀️ ⛅ 🌧️ Temp ....

Location / Park ....

Distance .... Duration ....

Trails ....

Elevation Gain / Loss ....

Terrain ....

Difficulty   Easy   1   2   3   4   5   6   Hard

Companions
....
....

Cost / Fees
....

Facilities
....

Cell Reception / Carrier ....

NATURE / WILDLIFE OBSERVED
....
....
....
....

Hiking rate ⭐ ⭐ ⭐ ⭐ ⭐

 # Hiking Notes

....

....

....

....

....

....

....

....

....

....

....

....

....

....

....

....

....

....

....

....

Hiking Notes

Date ....

Start Time .... End Time ....

Weather ☀ ☁ 🌧❄ Temp ....

Location / Park ....

Distance .... Duration ....

Trails ....

Elevation Gain / Loss ....

Terrain ....

Difficulty   Easy   1   2   3   4   5   6   Hard

Companions

....

....

Cost/ Fees

....

Facilities

....

Cell Reception / Carrier ....

NATURE / WILDLIFE OBSERVED

....

....

....

....

Hiking rate   ⭐ ⭐ ⭐ ⭐ ⭐

 # Hiking Notes

··
··
··
··
··
··
··
··
··
··
··
··
··
··
··
··
··
··
··
··
··
··

Hiking Notes

Date ....

Start Time .... End Time ....

Weather ☀ ☁ 🌧❄ Temp ....

Location / Park ....

Distance .... Duration ....

Trails ....

Elevation Gain / Loss ....

Terrain ....

Difficulty   Easy   1   2   3   4   5   6   Hard

Companions

....

....

Cost/ Fees

....

Facilities

....

Cell Reception / Carrier ....

NATURE / WILDLIFE OBSERVED

....

....

....

....

Hiking rate   ⭐ ⭐ ⭐ ⭐ ⭐

 # Hiking Notes

....

....

....

....

....

....

....

....

....

....

....

....

....

....

....

....

....

....

....

....

Hiking Notes

Date ....

Start Time .... End Time ....

Weather ☀ ☁ 🌧❄ Temp ....

Location / Park ....

Distance .... Duration ....

Trails ....

Elevation Gain / Loss ....

Terrain ....

Difficulty   Easy   1   2   3   4   5   6   Hard

Companions
....
....

Cost / Fees
....

Facilities
....

Cell Reception / Carrier ....

NATURE / WILDLIFE OBSERVED

....
....
....
....

Hiking rate   ⭐ ⭐ ⭐ ⭐ ⭐

Hiking Notes

Hiking Notes

Date ....

Start Time .... End Time ....

Weather ☀ ☁ 🌧❄ Temp ....

Location / Park ....

Distance .... Duration ....

Trails ....

Elevation Gain / Loss ....

Terrain ....

Difficulty   Easy   1   2   3   4   5   6   Hard

Companions
....
....

Cost / Fees
....

Facilities
....

Cell Reception / Carrier ....

NATURE / WILDLIFE OBSERVED

....
....
....
....

Hiking rate   ☆ ☆ ☆ ☆ ☆

Hiking Notes

Hiking Notes

Date ....

Start Time .... End Time ....

Weather ☀ ☁ 🌧 Temp ....

Location / Park ....

Distance .... Duration ....

Trails ....

Elevation Gain / Loss ....

Terrain ....

Difficulty   Easy   1   2   3   4   5   6   Hard

Companions
....
....

Cost / Fees
....

Facilities
....

Cell Reception / Carrier ....

NATURE / WILDLIFE OBSERVED

....
....
....
....

Hiking rate ⭐ ⭐ ⭐ ⭐ ⭐

Hiking Notes

....

....

....

....

....

....

....

....

....

....

....

....

....

....

....

....

....

....

....

....

....

....

....

Hiking Notes

Date ....

Start Time .... End Time ....

Weather ☀️ ☁️ 🌧️ Temp ....

Location / Park ....

Distance .... Duration ....

Trails ....

Elevation Gain / Loss ....

Terrain ....

Difficulty   Easy   1   2   3   4   5   6   Hard

Companions
....
....

Cost / Fees
....

Facilities
....

Cell Reception / Carrier ....

NATURE / WILDLIFE OBSERVED

....
....
....
....

Hiking rate ⭐ ⭐ ⭐ ⭐ ⭐

Hiking Notes

Hiking Notes

Date ....

Start Time .... End Time ....

Weather ☀ ☁ 🌧❄ Temp ....

Location / Park ....

Distance .... Duration ....

Trails ....

Elevation Gain / Loss ....

Terrain ....

Difficulty   Easy   1   2   3   4   5   6   Hard

Companions
....
....

Cost / Fees
....

Facilities
....

Cell Reception / Carrier ....

NATURE / WILDLIFE OBSERVED

....
....
....
....

Hiking rate ⭐ ⭐ ⭐ ⭐ ⭐

Hiking Notes

··
··
··
··
··
··
··
··
··
··
··
··
··
··
··
··
··
··
··
··
··
··
··

Hiking Notes

Date ....

Start Time .... End Time ....

Weather ☀ ☁ 🌧 Temp ....

Location / Park ....

Distance .... Duration ....

Trails ....

Elevation Gain / Loss ....

Terrain ....

Difficulty   Easy   1   2   3   4   5   6   Hard

Companions
....
....

Cost / Fees
....

Facilities
....

Cell Reception / Carrier ....

NATURE / WILDLIFE OBSERVED

....
....
....
....

Hiking rate   ⭐ ⭐ ⭐ ⭐ ⭐

Hiking Notes

Hiking Notes

Date ....

Start Time .... End Time ....

Weather ☀ ☁ 🌧 Temp ....

Location / Park ....

Distance .... Duration ....

Trails ....

Elevation Gain / Loss ....

Terrain ....

Difficulty   Easy   1   2   3   4   5   6   Hard

Companions
....
....

Cost / Fees
....

Facilities
....

Cell Reception / Carrier ....

NATURE / WILDLIFE OBSERVED
....
....
....
....

Hiking rate ⭐ ⭐ ⭐ ⭐ ⭐

Hiking Notes

Hiking Notes

Date ....

Start Time .... End Time ....

Weather ☀ ☁ ☔ Temp ....

Location / Park ....

Distance .... Duration ....

Trails ....

Elevation Gain / Loss ....

Terrain ....

Difficulty   Easy   1   2   3   4   5   6   Hard

Companions

....
....

Cost / Fees

....

Facilities

....

Cell Reception / Carrier ....

NATURE / WILDLIFE OBSERVED

....
....
....
....

Hiking rate   ⭐ ⭐ ⭐ ⭐ ⭐

Hiking Notes

Hiking Notes

Date ....

Start Time .... End Time ....

Weather ☀ ☁ 🌧 Temp ....

Location / Park ....

Distance .... Duration ....

Trails ....

Elevation Gain / Loss ....

Terrain ....

Difficulty   Easy   1   2   3   4   5   6   Hard

Companions

....

....

Cost / Fees

....

Facilities

....

Cell Reception / Carrier ....

NATURE / WILDLIFE OBSERVED

....

....

....

....

Hiking rate   ★ ★ ★ ★ ★

Hiking Notes

....
....
....
....
....
....
....
....
....
....
....
....
....
....
....
....
....
....
....
....
....
....

Hiking Notes

Date ....

Start Time .... End Time ....

Weather ☀ ☁ ☔ Temp ....

Location / Park ....

Distance .... Duration ....

Trails ....

Elevation Gain / Loss ....

Terrain ....

Difficulty   Easy   1   2   3   4   5   6   Hard

Companions
....
....

Cost/ Fees
....

Facilities
....

Cell Reception / Carrier ....

NATURE / WILDLIFE OBSERVED

....
....
....
....

Hiking rate   ⭐ ⭐ ⭐ ⭐ ⭐

Hiking Notes

Hiking Notes

Date ....

Start Time .... End Time ....

Weather ☀ ☁ 🌧❄ Temp ....

Location / Park ....

Distance .... Duration ....

Trails ....

Elevation Gain / Loss ....

Terrain ....

Difficulty   Easy   1   2   3   4   5   6   Hard

Companions

....

....

Cost/ Fees

....

Facilities

....

Cell Reception / Carrier ....

NATURE / WILDLIFE OBSERVED

....

....

....

....

Hiking rate   ⭐ ⭐ ⭐ ⭐ ⭐

Hiking Notes

....
....
....
....
....
....
....
....
....
....
....
....
....
....
....
....
....
....
....
....
....
....
....
....

Hiking Notes

Date ....

Start Time .... End Time ....

Weather ☀ ☁ 🌧❄ Temp ....

Location / Park ....

Distance .... Duration ....

Trails ....

Elevation Gain / Loss ....

Terrain ....

Difficulty   Easy   1   2   3   4   5   6   Hard

Companions

....

....

Cost / Fees

....

Facilities

....

Cell Reception / Carrier ....

NATURE / WILDLIFE OBSERVED

....

....

....

....

Hiking rate   ⭐ ⭐ ⭐ ⭐ ⭐

Hiking Notes

Hiking Notes

Date ....

Start Time .... End Time ....

Weather ☀ ⛅ 🌧 Temp ....

Location / Park ....

Distance .... Duration ....

Trails ....

Elevation Gain / Loss ....

Terrain ....

Difficulty   Easy   1   2   3   4   5   6   Hard

Companions
....
....

Cost / Fees
....

Facilities
....

Cell Reception / Carrier ....

NATURE / WILDLIFE OBSERVED
....
....
....
....

Hiking rate ⭐ ⭐ ⭐ ⭐ ⭐

 # Hiking Notes

Hiking Notes

Date ....

Start Time .... End Time ....

Weather ☀️ ☁️ 🌧️ Temp ....

Location / Park ....

Distance .... Duration ....

Trails ....

Elevation Gain / Loss ....

Terrain ....

Difficulty   Easy   1   2   3   4   5   6   Hard

Companions
....
....

Cost/ Fees
....

Facilities
....

Cell Reception / Carrier ....

NATURE / WILDLIFE OBSERVED

....
....
....
....

Hiking rate   ⭐ ⭐ ⭐ ⭐ ⭐

 # Hiking Notes

....

....

....

....

....

....

....

....

....

....

....

....

....

....

....

....

....

....

....

....

....

....

....

....

Hiking Notes

Date ....

Start Time .... End Time ....

Weather ☀️ ⛅ 🌧️ Temp ....

Location / Park ....

Distance .... Duration ....

Trails ....

Elevation Gain / Loss ....

Terrain ....

Difficulty   Easy   1   2   3   4   5   6   Hard

Companions
....
....

Cost / Fees
....

Facilities
....

Cell Reception / Carrier ....

NATURE / WILDLIFE OBSERVED

....
....
....
....

Hiking rate   ⭐ ⭐ ⭐ ⭐ ⭐

Hiking Notes

....
....
....
....
....
....
....
....
....
....
....
....
....
....
....
....
....
....
....
....
....
....
....
....
....

Hiking Notes

Date ....

Start Time .... End Time ....

Weather ☀ ☁ 🌧 Temp ....

Location / Park ....

Distance .... Duration ....

Trails ....

Elevation Gain / Loss ....

Terrain ....

Difficulty   Easy   1   2   3   4   5   6   Hard

Companions
....
....

Cost / Fees
....

Facilities
....

Cell Reception / Carrier ....

NATURE / WILDLIFE OBSERVED

....
....
....
....

Hiking rate   ⭐ ⭐ ⭐ ⭐ ⭐

Hiking Notes

Hiking Notes

Date ....

Start Time .... End Time ....

Weather ☀ ☁ 🌧❄ Temp ....

Location / Park ....

Distance .... Duration ....

Trails ....

Elevation Gain / Loss ....

Terrain ....

Difficulty Easy 1 2 3 4 5 6 Hard

Companions

....

....

Cost/ Fees

....

Facilities

....

Cell Reception / Carrier ....

NATURE / WILDLIFE OBSERVED

....

....

....

....

Hiking rate ⭐ ⭐ ⭐ ⭐ ⭐

Hiking Notes

Hiking Notes

Date ....

Start Time .... End Time ....

Weather ☀️ ☁️ 🌧️ Temp ....

Location / Park ....

Distance .... Duration ....

Trails ....

Elevation Gain / Loss ....

Terrain ....

Difficulty   Easy   1   2   3   4   5   6   Hard

Companions
....
....

Cost/ Fees
....

Facilities
....

Cell Reception / Carrier ....

NATURE / WILDLIFE OBSERVED

....
....
....
....

Hiking rate ⭐ ⭐ ⭐ ⭐ ⭐

Hiking Notes

....
....
....
....
....
....
....
....
....
....
....
....
....
....
....
....
....
....
....
....
....
....
....
....
....
....
....

Hiking Notes

Date ....

Start Time .... End Time ....

Weather ☀ ☁ 🌧❄ Temp ....

Location / Park ....

Distance .... Duration ....

Trails ....

Elevation Gain / Loss ....

Terrain ....

Difficulty   Easy   1   2   3   4   5   6   Hard

Companions
....
....

Cost/ Fees
....

Facilities
....

Cell Reception / Carrier ....

NATURE / WILDLIFE OBSERVED

....
....
....
....

Hiking rate   ⭐ ⭐ ⭐ ⭐ ⭐

Hiking Notes

Hiking Notes

Date ....

Start Time .... End Time ....

Weather ☀ ☁ 🌧❄ Temp ....

Location / Park ....

Distance .... Duration ....

Trails ....

Elevation Gain / Loss ....

Terrain ....

Difficulty   Easy   1   2   3   4   5   6   Hard

Companions
....
....

Cost/ Fees
....

Facilities
....

Cell Reception / Carrier ....

NATURE / WILDLIFE OBSERVED

....
....
....
....

Hiking rate   ⭐ ⭐ ⭐ ⭐ ⭐

 # Hiking Notes

Hiking Notes

Date ....

Start Time .... End Time ....

Weather ☀ ☁ 🌧❄ Temp ....

Location / Park ....

Distance .... Duration ....

Trails ....

Elevation Gain / Loss ....

Terrain ....

Difficulty   Easy   1   2   3   4   5   6   Hard

Companions
....
....

Cost / Fees
....

Facilities
....

Cell Reception / Carrier ....

NATURE / WILDLIFE OBSERVED

....
....
....
....

Hiking rate   ☆ ☆ ☆ ☆ ☆

 # Hiking Notes

Hiking Notes

Date ....

Start Time .... End Time ....

Weather ☀ ☁ 🌧❄ Temp ....

Location / Park ....

Distance .... Duration ....

Trails ....

Elevation Gain / Loss ....

Terrain ....

Difficulty   Easy   1   2   3   4   5   6   Hard

Companions
....
....

Cost / Fees
....

Facilities
....

Cell Reception / Carrier ....

NATURE / WILDLIFE OBSERVED

....
....
....
....

Hiking rate   ⭐ ⭐ ⭐ ⭐ ⭐

Hiking Notes

Hiking Notes

Date ....

Start Time .... End Time ....

Weather ☀ ☁ 🌧❄ Temp ....

Location / Park ....

Distance .... Duration ....

Trails ....

Elevation Gain / Loss ....

Terrain ....

Difficulty   Easy   1   2   3   4   5   6   Hard

Companions
....
....

Cost / Fees
....

Facilities
....

Cell Reception / Carrier ....

NATURE / WILDLIFE OBSERVED

....
....
....
....

Hiking rate   ⭐ ⭐ ⭐ ⭐ ⭐

Hiking Notes

Printed in Great Britain
by Amazon

50985252R00070